East Sussex
County Council

eastsussex.gov.uk

East Sussex Library and Information Services
Schools Library and Museum Service

D1349704

04360620 - **ITEM**

Capital Cities of the United Kingdom

Edinburgh

Anita Ganeri and Chris Oxlade

raintree
a Capstone company — publishers for children

Raintree is an imprint of Capstone Global Library Limited, a company incorporated in England and Wales having its registered office at 264 Banbury Road, Oxford, OX2 7DY – Registered company number: 6695582

www.raintree.co.uk
myorders@raintree.co.uk

Text © Capstone Global Library Limited 2017
The moral rights of the proprietor have been asserted.

All rights reserved. No part of this publication may be reproduced in any form or by any means (including photocopying or storing it in any medium by electronic means and whether or not transiently or incidentally to some other use of this publication) without the written permission of the copyright owner, except in accordance with the provisions of the Copyright, Designs and Patents Act 1988 or under the terms of a licence issued by the Copyright Licensing Agency, Saffron House, 6–10 Kirby Street, London, EC1N 8TS (www.cla.co.uk). Applications for the copyright owner's written permission should be addressed to the publisher.

Edited by Helen Cox Cannons
Designed by Philippa Jenkins
Original illustrations © Capstone Global Library Ltd 2016
Picture research by Eric Gohl
Production by Victoria Fitzgerald
Originated by Capstone Global Library Ltd
Printed and bound in China

ISBN 978 1 4747 2763 1
20 19 18 17 16
10 9 8 7 6 5 4 3 2 1

British Library Cataloguing in Publication Data
A full catalogue record for this book is available from the British Library.

Acknowledgements
We would like to thank the following for permission to reproduce photographs: Alamy: Andrew Wilson, 23, Gary Doak, 21, Russell Sneddon, 11, 22; Bridgeman Images: Valerie Jackson Harris Collection/© Look and Learn/Private Collection, 7; Capstone: Oxford Designer and Illustrators, cover (map), 1, 5; © Collins Bartholomew Ltd 2016. Reproduced with permission of HarperCollins Publishers: 28; iStockphoto: AlbertPego, 9, jmimages, 27; Newscom: Pictures Colour Library, 12, Polaris/Murdo MacLeod, 19, REX/ScottishViewpoint/PT-VS, 18, REX/Seconds Left/Andrew Fosker, 24; Shutterstock: Antonin Vinter, 16, Duirinish Light, 8, imagesef, 10, Jan Kranendonk, 26, JeniFoto, 4, Kyrien, 20, Leonid Andronov, 17, Mikadun, 6, Ross Strachan, 13, Songquan Deng, cover, 15, Zdenek Krchak, 14, 25.

Every effort has been made to contact copyright holders of material reproduced in this book. Any omissions will be rectified in subsequent printings if notice is given to the publisher.

All the internet addresses (URLs) given in this book were valid at the time of going to press. However, due to the dynamic nature of the internet, some addresses may have changed, or sites may have changed or ceased to exist since publication. While the author and publisher regret any inconvenience this may cause readers, no responsibility for any such changes can be accepted by either the author or the publisher.

EAST SUSSEX SCHOOLS LIBRARY SERVICE	
578872	
Askews & Holts	Nov-2016
941 GAN	£12.99

Contents

Where is Edinburgh? 4

The story of Edinburgh 6

Edinburgh today 8

Hills and a river 10

Edinburgh by the sea 12

The Royal Mile.................................... 14

Beautiful views.................................... 16

Museums and the zoo.......................... 18

Hidden gems 20

Shopping in Edinburgh 22

Sport in Edinburgh.............................. 24

Festivals and celebrations 26

Map of Edinburgh city centre 28

Glossary.. 29

Find out more 30

Places to visit..................................... 31

Index 32

Some words are shown in bold, **like this.**
You can find out what they mean by looking
in the glossary.

Where is Edinburgh?

Every country has a capital city. The capital is the most important city in that country. Edinburgh is the capital city of Scotland. The Scottish **Parliament** is in Edinburgh. The Parliament makes some of Scotland's laws.

Nearly 500,000 people live in Edinburgh.

4

This is a map showing where Edinburgh and Scotland are in the British Isles.

Edinburgh

SCOTLAND

NORTHERN IRELAND

REPUBLIC OF IRELAND

ENGLAND

WALES

Edinburgh became the capital of Scotland in 1437. It is the second biggest city in Scotland, after Glasgow. Most people in Scotland live in Edinburgh and Glasgow.

The story of Edinburgh

About 1,500 years ago, a local tribe built a **fort** on a rock. This is where Edinburgh Castle stands today. The fort was named "Eiden's burgh". This is where the name Edinburgh comes from.

There are many **medieval** buildings in the Old Town of Edinburgh.

In the past, thick smoke from fires often covered Edinburgh.

About 200 years ago, many factories and houses were built in Edinburgh. Smoke from coal fires in factories and houses choked the air. Edinburgh's nickname is "Auld Reekie". This means "Old Smokey" in Scots. The air is much cleaner today!

Edinburgh today

Today, Edinburgh is a big, busy city. People visit Edinburgh to go shopping and eat and drink in restaurants and cafés. Visitors can walk in the beautiful parks and look around old buildings and **monuments**.

More than 3 million people visit Edinburgh every year.

Many people live in beautiful buildings in Edinburgh's New Town.

Edinburgh's city centre is split into the Old Town and the New Town. There are many old buildings in the city. Because it has so many interesting buildings, the United Nations made Edinburgh a **World Heritage Site** in 1995.

Hills and a river

Edinburgh has lots of hills. Arthur's Seat, Castle Rock and Calton Hill are all famous hills in or next to the city. Arthur's Seat, in Holyrood Park, stands 251 metres high. It was once a live **volcano** that erupted 350 million years ago.

Walkers climb Arthur's Seat for a great view of the city below.

Dean Bridge is a famous old bridge over the Water of Leith.

The Water of Leith is a river that flows through Edinburgh. It flows very close to the city centre. Visitors can walk along the Water of Leith Walkway. It is possible to see herons, kingfishers and otters hunting for fish there.

Edinburgh by the sea

Edinburgh lies near a wide **estuary** called the Firth of Forth. This is where the River Forth flows into the North Sea. There are working **docks** in the area of the city called Leith.

You can go aboard The Royal Yacht *Britannia* at Leith.

Around 200 trains cross the Forth Rail Bridge every day.

There are four large bridges across the Firth of Forth, near Edinburgh. The Forth Rail Bridge was officially opened on 4 March 1890. It was the first major structure in the United Kingdom to be made of steel.

13

The Royal Mile

The Royal Mile is a famous street in Edinburgh. The Palace of Holyroodhouse and the Scottish **Parliament** building are at the bottom of the Royal Mile. The Queen stays at Holyroodhouse when she visits Edinburgh.

Many past kings and queens of Scotland lived at Holyroodhouse.

A gun is fired from Edinburgh Castle at one o'clock in the afternoon every day of the year.

Edinburgh Castle is at the top end of the Royal Mile. It was once the home of Scottish kings and queens. Inside the castle buildings are the Scottish **crown jewels** and a giant cannon, called Mons Meg.

Beautiful views

Calton Hill has some great views of the city. You can see Arthur's Seat, Edinburgh Castle and the Firth of Forth from there. There are also many **monuments** to see, including Nelson's monument.

Nelson's monument is shaped like Admiral Nelson's famous telescope.

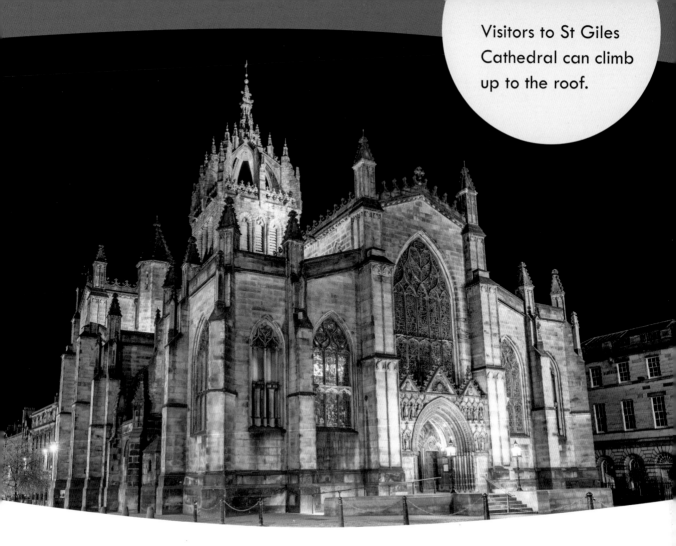

Visitors to St Giles Cathedral can climb up to the roof.

Edinburgh's most important church is the High **Kirk** on the Royal Mile. It is also named St Giles Cathedral. Inside, there are many beautiful **stained glass** windows. There is also a royal **pew** for the Queen.

Museums and the zoo

The National Museum of Scotland is in Edinburgh. It is a great place for finding out all about Scotland's fascinating past. You can learn about Scotland's rocks and **geology**, natural history, people and inventions.

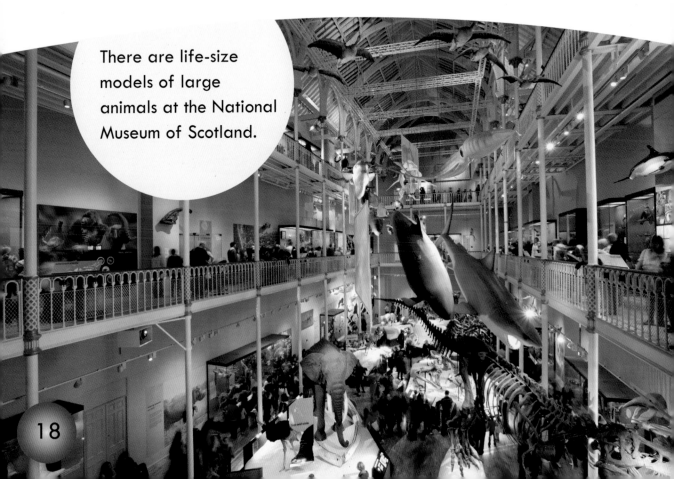

There are life-size models of large animals at the National Museum of Scotland.

The pandas are named Tian Tian (Sweetie) and Yang Guang (Sunlight). This is Yang Guang.

Edinburgh Zoo is a very popular place to visit. The most famous animals in the zoo are two giant pandas. The pandas arrived from China in December 2011. They are the only giant pandas in the United Kingdom.

Hidden gems

Close to Greyfriars **Kirk**, there is a statue of a small dog nicknamed Greyfriars Bobby. Legend has it that Bobby sat by his owner's grave when he died in 1858. Bobby stayed there for 14 years, until he himself died in 1872.

Touching Bobby's nose is said to bring good luck!

Mary King's Close is said to be haunted by the ghosts of the people who once lived there!

Mary King's Close is a maze of tunnels underneath the Royal Mile. The poor people of Edinburgh lived there until the 1750s. Then the streets were built over. You can visit Mary King's Close and see how people lived in those times.

Shopping in Edinburgh

Princes Street and George Street are two of Edinburgh's busiest streets. They are packed with shops and art galleries. Edinburgh's most famous shop is Jenners department store. It opened in 1838.

Jenners department store is a popular place for Christmas shoppers.

There is still a market in the Grassmarket every Saturday.

The Grassmarket is one of Edinburgh's oldest markets. It is more than 500 years old. Up until around 1670, people bought and sold cattle and horses there. After that it was used more as a goods market.

Sport in Edinburgh

Murrayfield Stadium is home to the Scottish rugby team. The city also has two big football clubs — Heart of Midlothian and Hibernian. They are known as Hearts and Hibs, for short.

The Scotland rugby team plays in dark blue.

The Edinburgh Marathon route goes past the Scottish **Parliament** building.

The Edinburgh Marathon is held in May each year. As many as 30,000 runners take part. They run through the middle of Edinburgh. Another famous race is the Seven Hills of Edinburgh Challenge. Runners have to climb all of Edinburgh's seven hills.

Festivals and celebrations

The Edinburgh Festival is one of the largest arts festivals in the world. There are hundreds of concerts, plays, films, comedy acts and children's shows. It takes place every August for three weeks.

Crowds flock to the Royal Mile to watch street performers.

There is a spectacular Hogmanay firework display above Edinburgh Castle.

Happy Hogmanay! The people of Edinburgh really know how to celebrate New Year's Eve. There is a giant, noisy party on Princes Street and fireworks at the Castle. Around 150,000 people go there to celebrate.

Edinburgh

©Collins Bartholomew Ltd 2015

400m
400 yds

Glossary

crown jewels crown and other jewellery worn by a king or queen

dock place where ships are built or where they are loaded and unloaded

estuary part of a river that meets the tide of the sea

fort building with strong walls that protects people inside from attack

geology study of minerals, rocks and soil

kirk Scottish word for church

medieval having to do with the period of history between AD 500 and 1450, called the Middle Ages

monument building or statue to celebrate a person or event

Parliament place where a country's laws are made

pew bench with a back to it that people sit on in church

stained glass coloured glass in a window

volcano place where molten rock comes out of the ground, or a mountain made from lava and ash

World Heritage Site natural or man-made site or area that is seen to be of international importance

Find out more

Books

I-SPY Edinburgh (Michelin Tyre PLC, 2011)

Let's Visit Scotland, Annabelle Lynch (Franklin Watts, 2015)

Time Out Edinburgh (Time Out Guides, 2015)

Websites

www.edinburghzoo.org.uk/webcams/panda-cam
Watch live videos of the pandas at Edinburgh Zoo!

www.ewht.org.uk
This site has plenty of photographs of Edinburgh's important historic buildings that are part of a World Heritage Site.

www.visitscotland.com/edinburgh
This is the official website of Visit Scotland, with lots of information on sights to see, places to eat and events.

Places to visit

Places mentioned in the book
Edinburgh Castle, Castle Hill, Edinburgh EH1 2NG
www.edinburghcastle.gov.uk

Edinburgh Zoo, Corstorphine Road, Edinburgh
EH12 6TS
www.edinburghzoo.org.uk

National Museum of Scotland, Chambers Street,
Edinburgh EH1 1JF
www.nms.ac.uk/national-museum-of-scotland

More places to visit
Camera Obscura and World of Illusions, Castlehill,
The Royal Mile, Edinburgh EH1 2ND
www.camera-obscura.co.uk

Dynamic Earth, Holyrood Road, Edinburgh EH8 8AS
www.dynamicearth.co.uk

Museum of Childhood, 42 High Street, Royal Mile
EH1 1TG
www.edinburghmuseums.org.uk/venues/museum-of-childhood

Index

Arthur's Seat 10, 16
"Auld Reekie" 7

Calton Hill 10, 16

Edinburgh Castle 6, 15, 16,
  27
Edinburgh Festival 26
Edinburgh Zoo 19
"Eiden's burgh" 6

festivals 26–27
Firth of Forth 12, 13, 16
Forth Rail Bridge 13

George Street 22
Grassmarket, the 23
Greyfriars Bobby 20

hills 10, 25
Hogmanay 27
Holyroodhouse, Palace of 14
Holyrood Park 10

map of Edinburgh city centre
  28

Mary King's Close 21
Mons Meg 15
Murrayfield Stadium 24

National Museum of Scotland
  18
New Town 9

Old Town 6, 9

Parliament, Scottish 4, 14, 25
population 4
Princes Street 22, 27

rivers 10, 11, 12
Royal Mile, the 14–15, 17,
  21, 26
Royal Yacht Britannia 12

Scottish crown jewels 15
shopping 8, 22–23
sport 24–25
St Giles Cathedral 17

Water of Leith 11

32